the CRY

poems of mourning sickness

by Tiffany Vakilian

Copyright © 2022 by Tiffany Vakilian

The Cry: Poems of Mourning Sickness

Designed by Square Tree Publishing: https://squaretreepublishing.com

Cover design by Sharon Marta: https://sharonmarta.com

Library of Congress Control Number: 2022912974

ISBNs:
Paperback/eBook: 979-8-9856148-1-7
Hardcover: 978-1-958978-17-7

Translated Title: *El Llanto: Poemas Sobre de Malestar Matutino*
Translated ISBNs
978-1-958978-06-1   Paperback
978-1-958978-07-8   eBook
979-8-9856148-2-4   Hardback

Speak Fire Publishing

All rights reserved, including the right of reproduction in whole or in part in any form, except for brief quotations embodied in critical articles or reviews.

Before We Begin

My heart has been breaking.
Breaking open, breaking down, breaking out, breaking through, breaking free.

The fruit of this process is highly personal, but strangely symbolic for a lot of universally shared pains. Through poetry and story, I can show you who I am. I invite you to understand how blessed I have been, despite how I walked the valley of the shadow of death. I invite you to learn how to love yourselves (and me) better with the honesty my words give you. I invite you to break with me.

Let us live beautifully with the holy light that shines through the areas some would call "less." We know it is more than telling, more than showing, more than sharing can ever say.

It is profound.
It is powerful.
It is here.

Foreword

Do you know the cry?

Accompanied with tears, first like rain misting, sprinkling, then flowing, and even flooding through an open window released from the internal rivers of the soul. We don't "know" things as they are; we "know" things as we are.

A perfect life is a myth, and we are all like smashed art pieces.

The surprising lesson Japanese Kintsugi art displays is, that in repairing the brokenness, there is a powerful message in the gold dust mixed with the glue! Kintsugi art doesn't hide the cracks but honors each wound by accentuating them with gold. They celebrate fractures as beautiful parts of the ceramic's story. Like the staggering beauty of every Kintsugi, we, too, can become even more treasured in our unique brokenness. But only when we are transparent and vulnerable can we allow the love and care of others to heal us.

The words you are about to read did not come from a mountaintop experience and the author paid a high price for them. They were hard-fought-for in the lowlands, in the wastelands of her soul. Do you know that cry?

Do you know what it is to have a precious son, daughter, or children who are a part of your heavenly cloud, though you wish you'd been able to kiss their breath this side of heaven? If not, do you know

someone who carries that cry within them?
I am acquainted with such grief.

My full-term-stillborn son, Patrick, left my womb on February 12, 1985. To this day, I remember in detail the events that changed me forever.

Do you know that cry?

Life is messy and full of delightful mysteries, frustrating predicaments, indescribable joy, and heart-wrenching suffering. Our human dilemma is to learn to dance between grief and joy; between the seen and unseen worlds. You can't find peace by avoiding life. And if you demand to understand why things happen as they do, you will forfeit the very peace you seek. The balm comes with seeking and trusting God and surpasses all understanding as it envelops you.

If a grain of wheat falls into the ground, it is no longer alone but multiplies into many seeds. Tiffany has bared her soul to us on this ground, carefully crafted from her cries into words that give birth from the depths of her spirit, soul, and body.

So, grave, where is your victory?

And death, where is your sting?

Kathleen O'Donnell Dew
Mother of Patrick O'Donnell
Author of *Divine Set-ups*
Dewnamis Ministries, Inc.
February 2022

Dedication

Dedicated to the ones who can't write about it, but who need to know that they were never alone in it. And for all those who died for me.

With so much, and love.

MOURN the way you need to.

Tiffany Vakilian

From my Journal, 2015

I was cleaning up around the house, planning to put up some images of peacocks in the guest bathroom. The peacock pictures kept rolling up, and I had no 6x18 frames for them. I opted to put them inside one of my thicker, heavier books.

The ultrasound photos rolled up too. Stupid paper. I put them there to be flattened until there was a frame or an album to bless. The photos were still there, not hiding. Waiting, I guess. But then I touched them, and a little tear in my heart came to bleed slightly. It had been a month. Pushing two.

Friends say it will stay with me forever. I am okay with that. Who wants such a beautiful wound to heal, really?

So now I wonder if I should go to counseling, because I must admit to feeling numb in some ways. I can fake it fairly well at times, when I step on the emotional landmines. It's almost laughable. Physically, I'm over the first and perhaps second hurdle. Still healing, but there's more testing and surgery to go. I'll leave getting my physical body to work right in the hands of the doctors for now. But professional help to get over my son? Unsure. How do I even discuss my son Moses' death? His never life? The never-was he was?

And who am I to be this sad? Of course, I should be. But I only am sometimes. It's confusing.

The Cry

In some ways, I admit, I am joyful. I mean, I am also devastated. And then again, I am honored. But mostly I am curious. And patient for the ways my son will send me messages from beyond the veil.

Thank you, Mo, for being in my cloud, though I so wish I'd been able to kiss your breath this side of heaven.

Tiffany Vakilian

A Little Quantum Time

Quickening hope and joy
But nostalgia hugs and holds on
A beautiful time to look
Back
Forward
At your feet
At your path
quickening hope and joy
Stones of remembrance
weigh on the heart
As the battle rages
on the field
And new life prepares
in the womb
Legacy
looms with prescient perfection
but nostalgia hugs and holds on
as the moment becomes infinite
so close to the veil
timelessness
in timeliness
timing is critical
hope and joy
quickening

The Cry

I Do

We didn't know
we thought it was the wedding glow
making me shine inside
outside
rain
sun
son
shine
hidden in the folds of me
watching daddy
adorn my fingers
this time in public
you had
best view in the wedding crew
we didn't know about you
but we were about to

Tiffany Vakilian

Eternal Perspective

"Love is not love which alters when it alteration finds…"

In my melanin is quantum time

Love often has skin on

History folds in on itself

I've heard worse

I've felt worse

I've done worse

And then I breathe in the peace

Because I am here

I am history

I am legacy

I am new

Love is a 4th dimensional principle

Quantum time is a leap of faith

My melanin is in it all

The Cry

Surprise

We sat in Hemet

At a favored buffet

excited and excited

Handing over the empty box

Celebrating a birthday joy

Surprise

Sharing our pregnancy

Surprise

They were so confused

And we laughed

when we corrected them

THE gift

Not in an empty box

Instead

Waiting

Inside my womb

The tears we shared

So full of joy

Like me

I don't regret the empty box; I regret how right it was.

Tiffany Vakilian

2015...

And then the pain came.

It was a Friday.

It was, I thought at first, a constipation cramp. The prenatal vitamins are apparently notorious for locking folks' bowels, as is pregnancy in general. But no. This was different. Pain sat there like flavoured evil, a pulsing stone, sending spikes down my right leg. It buzzed like a 3 a.m. alarm clock, pain ringing instead of sound.

Because I had just told my job I was pregnant (and then they fired me), Jesse had to call in some favors to update our health insurance. God's hand moved for sure, but that first attack of pain I had to endure at home without insurance cards. I didn't want to go to the ER, wait for four hours, then have them tell me that, due to my being pregnant, all they could give me was Tylenol.

I held down the couch that whole day.

Gramma came by to check on me and even made me some of her wonderful German potato salad. I'd been craving red meat and potatoes during the pregnancy, despite having an unconventional appetite my whole life. It was funny to me how I craved such "normal" things. To be fair, there was one night I asked Jesse to bring home shrimp and Cinnamon Toast Crunch.

Anyway, I ate and rested, and the next day I felt much better. I figured I would really have to watch my food, in and out, in order not to suffer that pain again.

The Cry

Pause

Hold up, wait a minute

I thought I was just beginning

About to do that new, good thing

But now I'm on pause

Like replacement strings

Hold up

Wait

One minute

All the markers must be finished

I'm not in this alone

And everyone has to find their way home

So I hold up

It's a long minute

But while I'm waiting

the world is still spinning

Dreams and aha's

Left and right

And some haters don't leave without a fight

As I hold up

Waiting minutes

Pause is practicing grace with new strength

Where it came from

I think I know

All this time I've been a seed sown

Tiffany Vakilian

And now
I
hold others up
While they
Hold up

The Cry

Go Deeper

You have to sometimes dip
and dip deep
I wanna do
but first I have to go through
Anointed heart, tongue, and pen
Again and again
Out of control
Wounds reopened for deep cleaning
Surgical the cuts
The rank funk of hopelessness
Anointed heart, tongue, and pen
Again and again
Helplessness—not helpful
And somehow beneficial to my soul
It is a great call
An honorable job
Bring up the skill level
To match the hands blessing us
Anointed heart, tongue, and pen
Again and again
Dive deep and expand my confidence
My comfort needs no voice
I'd rather be healed than clean
Dive in

Tiffany Vakilian

I'd like to introduce you to myself

Anointed

Heart

Tongue

Pen

The Cry

The Open Window

Golden times come to mind in the prime of Summer
Silly rhymes like rolling dimes are seeds in a field of sunflowers
Rain and heat, soft and sweet
Looking out the window
Bread and beer, there and here, burn in the heat of Summer
Family, friends, tight bonds and loose ends occurring upon the hour
Gift and gab, feeling fab
Looking in the window
Where did you go, how long has it been, questions rife in Summer
I've missed you so, oh how you've grown, loving reactions flutter
Come and visit before you miss it
Someone might close the window
Time is a genie, a beast, a bell, tolling the end of Summer
There are a million things to tell before the day melts like butter
The gift is the presence, even more than the lessons
My memory of that window

Tiffany Vakilian

2015...

That Monday, I called into the OB office. I told them that I knew I was supposed to wait until the referral was confirmed, but I was in just too much pain. They got me in that afternoon, praise God.

I got there in so much pain I could barely walk, let alone sit down. Everyone at Scripps OB in Encinitas was very accommodating. Ultrasounds and questions, paperwork and urine tests, almost a boring dance but for the pain and prognosis. Sally, the midwife who saw me that day, put me on Norco, a fairly strong narcotic, and told me that she wanted me back that Thursday to meet with Dr. F, the OB. My age didn't make the pregnancy as high-risk as the fibroids of unusual size eating up the space in my womb…

The Cry

Room Needed

I need a room

A golden room

Hot

I want it like an oven

Somewhere I can cook my feelings down into a roux

Something I can use to form me into myself

It is an old recipe

But with a lot of steps

My pride, salty

My guilt, oversweet

My griotte, rich but low in quantity

My purpose, undercooked

I need a room

A golden room

Where I can fall in love with myself

Yet again

And brand new

In a way that brings life to my babies

Where I can satisfy the pain of my un-shouted shouts

I need a room

And I need room

Big and small

Like words

More and less, please

Tiffany Vakilian

But still a golden room
Where I can lotion up my ashy dreams
Slather the gravy of heart
The legacy of my body
my race
my sex
my spirit
all of it
In a bright golden room
One of sun
and daughter and son
One I can float in like a river
Squeeze in like sexy boots
Where my body is justice
Where it just is
I need room
I need a room

The Cry

Burning Stones

There will always be fires

And

There will be stones

Consider:

Sometimes it burns only on the surface

heat and hurt

but nothing lasting

foolish almost

to give too much weight to

that pain

so gone

so yesterday

so eons ago

as you build

or

are built

And sometimes it melts down

hard places

into building blocks

into jewelry

into art

or into proof

just a proof

of staying power

Tiffany Vakilian

of survival

of the beauty of holding fast

"You didn't break me, fire"

the stone says

the stone stays

The stone stays

The Cry

Tiffany Vakilian

2015…

When Gramma found out I was on Norco, she went into a frenzy of worry, so much so that I had to tell her she was stressing me out. The Norco was a welcome relief, though the pain never went away completely. I could feel when the drug wore off. The pain climbed up my spine as if roused from sleep.

I went through 30 pills in one week…

The Cry

Untitled

I met an echo
It lived in me
A murky possibility of time destiny
Now and infinity
But I didn't know I was touching the outside of time
When I rested my hand on my belly
Outside the womb
Outside the veil
You came through, but only on the outside
Only an echo

2015…

Pain was like a bully, trying to get at me from whatever crack or crevice I laid open. It was agony…

The Cry

Rain on a Leaf

I am a leaf in the rain
Poured over, made clean
I am shining and pristine
Like morning glory all day
I am a tree in the storm
Sometimes palm, cedar, oak
Even if cut down, I stoke
The fires where I can
I am a mighty one
I pour love from whence it comes
This conduit has begun
To understand her destiny
You are a treasure too
I don't need to be just like you
Keep doin' what YOU do
Let the rain fall on you

Tiffany Vakilian

What I Can Carry

You never know what it is someone is carrying or how they are dispersing that load throughout their souls.

I can't say with any certainty that any of us are doing it right, and the idea that some are doing it better is just asking for acid to be poured on.

There are Joys to carry. There are burdens. There are reminders. There are Legacies.

When you know you are being carried, do you wonder about what you carry? When you are carrying someone, do you consider what they bring along for the ride?

So much connection is based on burden, but then, so much connection is based on strength.

Ask…

Beg the question

What do you carry?

What do I carry?

What can you carry?

What can I carry?

The Cry

Tiffany Vakilian

2015...

There was never any genuine relief. The pain kept me up at night, which zapped my energy during the day. I lost my appetite, forcing myself to eat when all I wanted was to be free from the pain.

Blood tests, urine tests, a 24-hour urine collection, and no relief in sight. I met with Dr. F, a tall, older man with a little gold cross peeking out of his doctor coat. He was matter of fact, but still kind as he told me his concerns. I remember how the timbre of his tone was consistent, and not too deep. He'd given talks like this before. I stared at the cream-colored walls as he talked about what was going on inside. My kidneys were allowing too much protein into my urine—something called proteinuria. And the fibroids were huge. I was 13 weeks, but the primary care physician thought I was 25 before I went to see Dr. F, who referred me to Dr. T for a Level 2 ultrasound. It was in a building about fifty yards away, and I felt I could make it without moving the car.

I walked into the new building and took the elevator to the lower level. It was a steel-colored day, and the rain blew through the nape of my neck, chilly and irritating. I had my cool umbrella, the white one with the Michonne-inspired Katana handle, but I opted to leave it in the car. I wished later that I'd brought it, if only to use it as a weight bearing cane. I got a little turned around, but eventually found the lower level of the building. I'll never forget how pretty the foliage was as I looked up through the windows. It was hopeful, in a melancholy

The Cry

way. The office foyer was a cave, so fitting with the emotions of the day, and the matching weather. When I went into the room for the ultrasound, I almost felt I'd gone underwater, and the dark depths were only brightened by the images on the screen. After it was done, I'd gone back to the "cave entrance" and sat, waiting for the results under yellow wall sconces.

Dr. T, the perinatologist, was taller and thinner than Dr. F, but he said basically the same things. The fibroids were causing all of my pain and making the likelihood of preterm labor and a C-section birth more than likely. As we were discussing things, I had what I called a "pain spasm" in the perinatologist's office, where a rusty dagger shot up through my womb, trying to reach the crown of my head. My whole body seized up, and I failed to stifle the whisper of agony. The wail fought back, climbing my throat like a muted tea kettle and stealing my ability to speak. The perinatologist offered to admit me to ER. I took a Norco in front of him as I battled my own body. I won, but that too exhausted me. I should've let him admit me, but I just wanted to go home. Was that stupid of me? After all that time in the perinatologist's office measuring my fibroids and trying to find out the sex of the baby, I just wanted to get to my bed and try to Norco the pain away...

Tiffany Vakilian

The devil Comes

He comes to wreck me so I will stay silent

Someone needs pages to cry into

All alone at 3:20 in the morning

Trying to be strong while muscles are shaking from overuse

Losing power

He comes to distract, which is thievery of passion

And I burn with the healing from the hurt

All alone at 3:21 in the morning

I let the tears fall inside my heart, inside the text

Gaining rest

He comes and I can't find the will to fight

But I cry out in my pages, "God help me!"

And the peace is a rushing, ringing, wind

I'm not alone, even at 3:22 in the morning

And *victory* is proclaimed

Over he who comes

The Cry

Tiffany Vakilian

2015…

Every time I heard my little Buttbutt's heartbeat, or saw him moving about on the ultrasound screen, my heart would leap for hope, and often I would cry. Buttbutt's heartbeat was always strong, and it was difficult to find him sitting still. Pastor Mike said he had "boogie fever," and I was always giggling about how "Buttbutt was dancin' too much." I prayed and I told God that I'd endure all the pain for my baby.

The pain got worse, and I had to get a Norco refill. I was supposed to see Dr. F that Friday, and I'd made it a point to talk to him about other options for the pain. I was already 16 weeks, but my stomach was so much bigger. The various doctors were always questioning my due date. 7/17, 7/20, 7/23, 7/27—they settled on 7/20, but not with any real certainty. I was 16 weeks, but I measured at closer to 27. And the pain would not relent…

The Cry

Outside Air

The best laid plans are never the expectation fully realized
Even on their best day
In no way
Is the plan better than the reality walked out
Walk about
Try it out
There is a reason to sometimes cry it out
Because life is not memory
And plan is not reality
When you grow the tree
Which is technically
Some still, sacrificed, dead seed
You had to put it in the ground
Let it do what it do
With no one else around
No likes on Facebook
No Tweets
No Gram
No outside air in which to go H.A.M.
No mosquitos or birds
Just dreams and words
Sometimes you come out slow
But that is what it is like to grow
Your mountaintop gives a great view

Tiffany Vakilian

But only to those up there with you
Some folks still got climbin' to do
I'm not that mountain there
I'm climbing up my own set of stairs
Graveled up
To level up
Tears sometimes
Go with the mishmashed rhymes
Storytellin' on my soul
Breathing outside air
Fighting off old trolls
I plan, God laughs, then we take a stroll
Out in the outside air

The Cry

Tiffany Vakilian

Friday, February 6, 2015

Mom was running late. I called her, texted. But she arrived five minutes after we were supposed to be at Dr. F's office. Her RA flared up for the first time in weeks, and she caught some slow traffic. I tried to maintain my calmness, but I got upset that we were about to be late. While we were in the car, I let her have it for not communicating the hindrances she was dealing with. She took my thoughts and gave me some of her own. We got to the office at 8:40. We were supposed to arrive at 8:15 for the appointment at 8:30. It was the hand of God that made them let us into the appointment. Mom dropped me off at the door and then went to park the car.

Dr. F came in, and the first thing he did was let me listen to the heartbeat. It was so strong it plucked my heart like a guitar, and I almost cried out for joy. I LOVE that sound.

Mom came in, and Dr. F showed us a book with images of fibroids. He explained that mine were "just massive" and that unfortunately my pregnancies would continue to be painful ones. "50/50 chance," he said. I said, "Day by day," and he agreed. His hope was that I'd make it to 27 weeks, while being "cautiously optimistic" that I'd make it that far, with 90% chance of a C-section birth and 100% chance of visiting my baby in the Neonatal Intensive Care Unit until released.

And then I was sent for more blood tests. Mom sat with me like a champ and even managed to run into someone she knew. She talked

The Cry

to them while I was in the lab, and when I walked out, we made lunch plans. We made a brief stop at Walmart. Walking continued to be excruciating, and I would squat when the pain got out of control. We drove in Mom's new Kia, and I told her about Jose's Tacos near the Home Depot I needed to visit.

Mom was so nice, despite her rough morning and my pregnant rudeness. She kept dropping me off near the entrances so I wouldn't have to walk so far. When we went to Home Depot, I got out and walked behind the car.

It felt like a balloon burst between my thighs. Instantly, I was soaked from my crotch to my knees. Thank God Mom hadn't pulled off. I franticly motioned for her to put her window down. When she did, I said, "Mom! Wait! My water just broke!"

Tiffany Vakilian

The Cry

If I could make
the sound
clawing its way up
from the bottom of my soul
If I could quantify it
define it
release it
spell it
That would be the title of my book
But that "word"
That sound
that cry
is too powerful
too deep
too beautiful
authentic
raw
full of joy
full of torture
it can't even fit to come out of my mouth
let alone reach your ears

The Cry

Quickly Now

This door is open
Quickly now,
walk on through it
Leave the past to grow.

Tiffany Vakilian

February 6...

We got back in her car and zoomed to TriCity ER, as I could see it adjacent to the Home Depot parking lot. It wasn't right next door, but it was less than a mile away. I soaked Mom's car-seat during that brief drive, but thankfully it was only water. I walked in crying, but calm. It was as if something cushioned my brain the moment the water came down and out of me. Maybe I was in shock. It was a peace in the midst of the pain and nerves.

When they admitted me and put me in a wheelchair, it was the first relief from the pain I'd had in weeks. When they helped me to undress, there was so much blood. They asked me if I was in pain, but it was gone. I called Jesse from Mom's phone on the drive over, and it was one of the rare times he answered at work. He showed up nervous and teary-eyed.

They inserted an IV. They drew blood. They gave me a pelvic exam. The doctor (or technician) saw one of the fibroids and part of my cervix. The ER technician/OB said that there appeared to be bits of amniotic sac inside what he could see of my cervix. "If you haven't already had the miscarriage, it is unfortunately a 90% chance you will soon."

They took me for a sonogram. Jesse had arrived by that time and heard the horrible news. He came with me down the halls to the imaging room. Two women were there, and Jesse held my hand as

The Cry

they began. They performed the ultrasound pretty much silently. We were smiling, almost, when we entered Ultrasound 2, but as they took to their work, the room lost color. The quieter they became, the grayer I saw the room become. When we got back to the room, the skinny blonde said, "I'm sorry for your loss."

That was the second devastation.

I found myself back in pain, so the nurse on duty gave me Dilotid. It felt like someone gently seized all the muscles in my neck and then just pushed my head two inches up, while traveling down my spine, one vertebra at a time, shutting them off like light switches. Time became relative.

I had to pee after a while. They gave me a bed pan, but nothing happened. I'd already done it twice. I felt it like a dam about to, albeit slowly, break. A trickle is all I wanted, but though I tried, I couldn't make a single drop come out. I asked Jesse to help me sit up so I could push.

It felt like another pop, with reverse suction. My eyes went wide, and I said calmly but immediately, "Push the button." I knew what had come out of my body. Who had come out.

I'd given birth.

Slick. Slippery. Easy release like a popped eardrum. I never thought to look at the time. Armageddon of a failure there. Or perhaps a blessing of ignorance. I just started crying and saying no over and over and over. Jesse held me as I turned to the wall in our fine, overfull room. The IV hung on a nail in the wall because there was no room for the normal apparatus and my bed, the blood pressure machine, Mom and Jesse in their chairs, a tiny sink and cupboard, and another cart with pelvic exam items which they left in the room.

There were only my tears in place of breath. Time stopped, restarted, stared at me as I pulled myself into the brokenness of the moments.

It was sensation. Tears. Fabric. Liquid. Pressure from Jesse's arms around me.
The ER doctor came back, and then the nurse. I didn't want it to be true, but that didn't change a thing. When the doctor came in, I looked at him and said something to the effect of, "I think I just gave birth."

The OB came shortly after. "I want to see him," I stated starkly, scared they would do something with the remains and I wouldn't get to kiss him goodbye. Everyone who walked in was so quiet, trying to move in and out of our heartbreak like servants. Was it a kindness? Were they afraid? Was it their policy to be so silent after, trying to be respectful?

After a time they cleaned up our little one and the OB confirmed what I knew. "It's a boy."

The Cry

I Didn't Know

I knew it would be hard
They seemed to laugh when they told me about the fibroids
I thought it was a good thing, almost
They took so much blood
But the fibroids grew
I know it wasn't my fault
But was there anything more I could have done?
Anything to save you at all?

                You were the holiest gift
                    Too holy maybe
           Is that why you poured out of me like blood?

Tiffany Vakilian

Shut In

You needn't believe
in the power of sunlight
but I do
I have held
bloody masses
in my hand
and while I don't attribute
that issue of blood
to the lack of sunlight
I know this to be true
had I not opened my windows
today
I would have stayed in
in fear of blood and clots
and the poetry in my head is too fragile
too fragile
like the child in my body
Becoming stronger and stronger
opening up to the sun
like a window
like a womb
and the blood
like an open wound
means less and less

The Cry

than the sunshine

in my hope

and coming through the window

Oh yes, I believe in the power

of the sun

and I am open to the light

and the life

that comes

Tiffany Vakilian

Bury My

Bury my scalp
with a shroud of love
In a sweet folding
layer upon layer
Bury my head
deep in the ground
Let no light be found
This growth must be done in the dark
My eye, my teeth,
my skin, my soul
No one sees
No one knows
Bury my hands
with no twine, no binding
They have work to do
in the depths
I'm weaving something
Warp to weft
This too must be done in the dark

The Cry

Tiffany Vakilian

February 6…

We were all faucets turning on and off. They kept bringing us tissues until, just before they admitted me and took me to labor and delivery, they found a huge stash in the lower cupboard.

They cleaned up our child and presented him to us in a white towel. He barely would have fit in my hand from the base of my palm to the tip of my middle finger. This little person in my hand had a strong, sure heartbeat not six hours earlier. I'd heard it, twice. Now he lay there with eyes that never had a chance to open and see outside the womb. They were still sealed shut at 16 weeks. He had his hands and feet, his little penis. I kissed his tiny head, which felt like cool plastic, and was the color of the center of a rose. He had no skin yet.

…His name is Moses. Was Moses. Is Moses. I think I traumatized myself by staring at him for so long. But there was a grace to his tiny symmetry. I couldn't not hold him, my little one. I'd been holding him for the last 16 weeks while he danced all around my womb. I still feel his little pokes. Was that what they were calling "flutters"? He already had a sense of humor, my little guy, trying to tickle me from the inside. Maybe he was sending me messages.

They left us blessedly alone for around an hour…

The Cry

The Day You Came

Mom was driving
I was in pain
I was angry
I was in pain

We were late
You were early
Us by minutes, you by months
I was in pain

Walking hurt
Waiting hurt
Medication failed me
I was in pain

And there
Right outside Home Depot
My body failed me
Relief, and then a new pain

I had to walk into ER
You falling out the bottom
They were almost fast
I wasn't in pain

Tiffany Vakilian

You were so soft
Sliding around and then out
Already gone, I didn't want to believe
I wasn't in pain

The ultrasound confirmed
What we knew
I kissed your red body goodbye
I will never fully explain that pain

The Cry

Skeleton Tee

I wrapped you in grey

One red heart

Celebrating your coming bones

But not like I ended up

Celebrating your bones

I wanted to feel your heart

Your hiccups

Your hand holding mine

Instead I feel cotton

It is soft

Ethereal compared to your fingers

I bought the shirt as a joke

And now it feels like

Maybe I always knew

And that skeleton

Connects me to you

Tiffany Vakilian

February 6…

…It seemed so simple a thing when she packed him up and took him away. I still didn't know what time it was. I don't even know if Jesse was still holding my hand. I remember the pain had returned with a vengeance, as if it were mad that I had other things to focus on. It stole my focus at every possible step.

Dr. M was a tall, dark man with the bedside manner of a dump truck held by a two-year-old. Apparently, he was on call. As he entered my room and sat down, he told us he ordered Fentanyl due to my "low tolerance for pain." My exhausted hackles went up listening to him, SO thoughtless and uncaring. But the placenta was still in my body and had to come out before infection set in. They were going to do that right there, in the room, by hand. With help of a nurse, he pulled down an enormous light hidden in a ceiling panel. Once they turned it on, Dr. M sat down to the right of the foot of my bed and unceremoniously tried to remove my placenta with two fingers and a set of sponge forceps.

Pain shot through me, and I screamed. Despite myself, and my drugged state, I scooted up the bed, away from Dr. M and the pain. Should I slap him if he comes near me again? There was no drug that could make that pain less demonic. I felt bad for the women celebrating their births in the nearby rooms. As if reading my mind, Jesse grabbed my hand, but I still pulled away from Dr. M, who now embodied all things evil.

The Cry

"Bear with me. Bear with me," he kept saying as he probed my womb for my placenta. We weren't sure, but I just knew it was resting behind one of the upper fibroids. Barely a moment's breath and Dr. M's fingers attacked me like my body had become a nuclear bomb detonator pipe organ. Dr. M had longish hair and a thick accent I couldn't place, but I didn't notice any of it at the time. All I could think of was the white blazing pain blasts leaving ash trails at the bottom of my soul. I couldn't escape them. They were all inside of me.

"Stop! Just stop!" I said, two decibels above a whisper but with a shaking head and straining arms pulling away. He heard me, thank God. He removed his hands and, in an attempt to "help," tells me of the fire-walkers, who walk on glass shards and nails, and how they were all successful because they put their minds from the pain. He also gave me the option of being anesthetized so that he could remove the placenta surgically. I was 75% for the surgery when I think Jesse said to give it one more try. He was right there with me. I could try one more time if he was there. But I needed a minute to prepare and said as much. I also requested a pillow to bite and scream my escaping soul into. I knew I'd need to catch it in something before it ran out of the room.

I took Jesse's hand, now understanding what that word "forever" meant to me. He fastened me to him. I nodded my readiness, and Dr. M began again.

I must admit, telling him when to start and knowing what would happen helped to lessen the pain. So did Jesse telling me to look into his eyes. But how does one lessen a bomb detonation once it's started? I still felt the blast wave echo through me, ripping screams of pain that I grunted into the pillow. I tried hard not to pull away. I tried.

Dr. M could not get my placenta out. He conceded defeat and told me I'd be having surgery. It felt like an abandoned building rested inside my crotch.

Tiffany Vakilian

Low Tolerance

"Your tolerance for pain is low," he said
Thinking he had context
As he reached inside and around 13 fibroids
Attached to my womb
It was impossible not to cry out
Emotionally exhausted before his torture
My adrenaline spiked as he set the tools to work
Up
Inside
Around
Not far enough
He couldn't get the amniotic sac
He couldn't see
How it was attached
To my womb
To the foreign bodies
It wouldn't come out
I screamed
I am still screaming

The Cry

Tiffany Vakilian

February 6…

Time passed again. I was told surgery would be fairly quick, like 10-15 minutes, but the OB had to perform an emergency C-section before he could get to me. I also found out that I'd be leaving Labor and Delivery and going to the Pavilion, which was basically going from solitary to gen-pop. But I honestly didn't feel like I deserved to stay in Labor and Delivery. I didn't have a baby to join me…

The Cry

Post-crash Burning (From February 2015):

Can't

Or

Shouldn't

Keep or share this chapter

Ashes can draw the fiery wings

Dampened

Or

More perhaps

Bread with faulty yeast

Supposed to be rising

But it isn't as fast as it "should" be

Release

Or

Forgive the self

For things outside of one's control

It is rising slowly

The trajectory—now so gloriously weighted

Ambition

Or

Someone's expectation

My own perhaps, set too high

She's supposed to try to fly again

And he has to let himself

Tiffany Vakilian

Seed

Or

Unexpected harvest

Didn't expect this garden to grow

It's ok if you tend my ground

As I grapple with my new flight plan

~~~ ~~~ ~~~

It is a strange time in my life right now. But in a new and different way.

The Cry

Untitled

I think of you sometimes when I look at your brother and sister. What of you do I see in them? How would you have led them into or out of mischief?

And yet, I flip the coin and I'm glad you aren't here. One less person I have to explain this world to. One less Black man to fear for. Is that bad? Being happy that you were spared?

I would have loved you falling asleep on me.

I would have hated your blood spilling for *any* reason.

I would have loved hearing your voice.

I would have hated teaching you how to be silent to stay alive.

I am exhausted from flipping the coin of what I have told myself to feel about your being or not being here.

Tiffany Vakilian

February 6…

…Pop-Pop came in and sat down, grabbing my hand like he was on a boat pulling loose from the moorings. I had nothing to say. My own ship was out to sea. Gramma laughed nervously at her flowery submission, apologizing for its Valentine theme and glittery red heart sticking out. I really didn't mind it…

The Cry

There There, Heart

Hold to me, heart

Beat so hard

Break the world

Again

Again

Learning again

Remembering again

Crying to the tune of time

And tell yourself again,

"There there, now…"

It's a heavy thing

But you shall beat

And beating back chaos

Your rhythm is exposed

And still subtle

Hold to me

Again

"There there…"

Tiffany Vakilian

Seeing in the Dark

This grassy blackness feels fibrous under the fingers.
It reeks of old things, but now the perspective sees fertile soil.
I wish and wonder while my fingers wander into this ground.
This is a draft.
I am a
first round.
Maybe a second or even a third.
Who knows?
But the darkness feels good.
Before it felt lonely.
The darkness doesn't feel silent.
Now, it feels ready.
I'm coming alive in the death I thought had claimed me.
This wasn't even a death.
This was more a
getting over myself.
I can give more.
But it won't look the same.
I can ask for more.
I understand the value of my value.
I can push and shove because I understand a tiny bit more of my weaponry.
Holding my voice sacred.
Not taking it for granted.

The Cry

It looks a lot more like quiet.
I'm feeling a new height in this deep.
And this unburying earth feels like I still have potential.
I wonder what that will realize if I just till the soil?

Tiffany Vakilian

You Are Not Made of Stone

Blackbird, fly. You are not made of stone.
All around you is proof of life. Write this down. Say it out loud. You are not made of stone.
It's okay to feel the bad feelings. The childish feelings. You will never see perfection this side of heaven. And you are not made of stone.
How does that Blackbird fly? Very well, because she's Mine. I gave you Phoenix dragonfly wings, in son-shined-through-brilliant colors. And you are not made of stone.
You want to tell them all how beautiful they are. How marvelous. How beloved. That's because you see them more with My eyes than you see yourself.
Spell it right, spell it wrong. You are NOT made of stone.
Blackbird, fly. Shine. Be all sides of what I have given you. Unfurl your wings and sing every note I've given you. Your heart IS a heart of flesh, and you are not alone with me in your wilderness. I gave you people to walk with. To fight with. To be loved by. You are beloved and you are good. You are righteous, and you are NOT made of stone.
Feel it. Feel it all. Go after that dream. And smile with your cello-shaped body. It's Yours. I gave it to you. It is more than just skin, muscle, and bone. You are a healed, whole thing. You are not made of stone.
Blackbird, fly. Your wings are no more clipped than the ocean is held back. Breathe THAT in. Speak it out. You are NOT made of stone.
You are Mine. Made of love. Made of prophecy. Made to love. Made to

The Cry

prophesy. You are not made of stone.
You are made of My blood. My flesh. I broke for you on your nastiest day. And here we are. Stand in your power, my princess. My child. My blackbird. Fly.
Because you are not made of stone.

Tiffany Vakilian

February 6…

…I'd convinced Jesse to go home, to take some items and bring back my blue bowed cap. He was hilariously macho, managing to grab at least five handle-free bags, a bouquet of flowers and a tray of cookies, sandwiches, and drinks (with all the condiments) in one trip.

One of the ladies from my church named Mary got the news from someone, most likely a text. She'd come to sit shiva perhaps, but her timing was such that she arrived just as we were leaving. She walked down to surgery prep and stayed until they rolled me out of surgery, back into post-op. Jesse arrived with my hat, which somehow made me feel more protected. Mary said good night, and Jesse came with me to my new room in the pavilion. Changing of the guard. In my new room, I managed some conversation with Jesse, and we talked until around one in the morning when they kicked him out. The nurses were kind about it. But it was good just talking to him quietly in our half of the room. We planned to get a dog, heal from the surgery, get the fibroids removed, heal from that, and then have twins.

The Cry

To the Men

We see you
the in and out of our heartbreak
can sometimes blind us
to the fact that
this black hole
is yours in every way
we see you
put on the mask
please show us the door
so we can go with you
we want to
dive in it together
because for so long
you held the line
silent while we screamed
when we could scream
but now we want to make room
and tell you
we SEE you

Tiffany Vakilian

2015...

I couldn't sleep with the IV tube in my arm and on a foreign bed without Jesse, but I dozed off every hour or so between pain medication requests and bathroom trips. I did speak a little to the woman sharing the room with me, and I got a sponge bath which was awkward, though I felt markedly more human afterward. I was able to eat breakfast, but it didn't satisfy.

I wanted to go home…

The Cry

Feelings

I dragged myself around
Duty bound to keep feelings down
No one knew what to do
With their feelings

My laughs were honest but
Most of my heart was shut
There's no "snapback" framework
for these feelings

Until I finally said,
"No, I'm nowhere near ready yet,"
My husband was able to get
in touch with my feelings

And then we began
Me as woman, he as man
to replant the burning land
of our feelings

Tiffany Vakilian

Prolificness

I have been sitting on this guilt.
Feelin' SO bad, y'all.
Holding this guilt like a stock gain in my bank account.
How about my algorithm with that guilt?
It was impossible to speculate.
I have to let go of it.
I have been eating cancerous thoughts of hurting, weighty feelings.
It burned as it went down.
It cut.
And I kept taking it in.
A new flavor.
The same guilt.
But then…
But God…
The Lord held up my chin and told me, "You're prolific."
"How?" I asked Him.
"In the work you do."
"Huh?"
Really?
Is that all?
Is that
okay?
Can my land be married?
Desolate to prolific?

The Cry

YES.

I am releasing my timeline.

I am releasing my guilt.

And none of my given talents will ever be buried.

So, how 'bout yes.

How 'bout I stop seeing the timeline and just walk the road?

How about yes?

Yes, to the work.

Yes, to the prolificness.

Tiffany Vakilian

I Feel You

I feel you, art. I feel you moving through my heart, in between my breath and giving no quarter. It hurts, and it sings, and it makes me give up sleep and cry for the beauty of it all. I feel you, pushing me so far outside my comfort zone, I forget where home is. Let me smile at the cream and sugar of you. Let me cry at the diamond glittering in the sea of you. How lucky am I to have you inside me, so dark chocolate brown. It feels so good to feel you, art. The life you give me. The hard work you make me do. You have always been my truest friend and most ride-or-die ally. You cussed all them haters out when I was crying. And you told me not to. You handled it, defending me in the dark. You, art, I know. You, art, I trust. You are God's gift, and most intimately mine.

I feel you.

The Cry

Truth Melts Magic

Truth melts magic
and there is no voice stronger
it hides sometimes
but cannot be denied
Truth melts magic
like old music in a gramophone
singing songs not yet written
because those meant to write them are still
too scared to open their throats
Truth melts magic
it rages in silence
silencing rage
tickling neglect and opening that long forgotten
holy forged weapon
Truth melts magic
and every time I see
I cry
at yet another lie I've been living
ripping open, ripping free
Daring
to be true
not just magical

Tiffany Vakilian

The Funny Thing About Joy

No one told me I would have joy
As my son lay dead in my arms
My broken heart, red and lifeless as his little body
But I knew there was a way back
And it would find me
Joy don't look like shiny days
Though most people see it there
Joy rests in the restless nights
Where prayer is the breath keeping you alive
Where you walk to the fridge
To get a drink
And the devil meets you there with suicidal thoughts
Joy found me when I was afraid to be alone
Joy waited for me to want to want to
Joy didn't lie about the work to be done
Joy stood by like a sentinel
As I was cut and bled, parts removed
As I was scarred and healed
As I tried and failed
And failed
And failed
And joy was there when the seed was planted
Joy shouted in the silent room
The day the blood came, but my daughter survived

The Cry

Joy was with me when I was scared to give birth

And forced to rest in bed

While the devil plotted to take both me and my unborn hope

And family and friends abandon you

Because they didn't know how to grieve with you

Joy made me smile

Dared me to talk about the unspeakable

Infant loss

Details taboo to others

His tiny body

His red skin

My pregnancy again

And again

The funny thing about Joy

Was its staying power in my weakness

And then my new, strange, shift

Joy asked nothing of me

But left an open hand for me to take

When I was brave enough to brace myself

Crazy enough to try again

To believe in my power to create

And create Joy

Tiffany Vakilian

2015…

…Before I knew it, I was home. People came by. People brought food. People prayed. The sun came up and went down. Time passed…

The Cry

To The Friends I've Lost Through Infant Loss

It's a rather horrible link you've given yourself

To consider helping share my grief as a bad omen

Beyond your ability to cope

To reach out

To rebuild

We all grieve differently

But I didn't think your grieving would look

So much like cowardice

So much like running

That fickle natured superstition

That gives loneliness to combat loneliness

Maybe I am being too hard on you

But it didn't happen to you that day

And I didn't run from you

Even when I had the chance(s)

I've tried to make a comfy space for you to come back

I keep the door open a bit

But I can't say for sure I want you there anymore

Waiting for the next shoe to drop

So you can break my trust and abandon me

Again

Only God can fix what broke between us

Tiffany Vakilian

Moss, Bush, Dwarf, Mighty

Walking out forgiveness is like growing a forest from the very first seed in the dirt.
I wish I could say it is easy, and there won't be bloody days, weeks, months—years. But there is truth in the blood. In the tears. There can even be joy in the holy depths of rejections, even self-rejections. The people who see you, or actively deny seeing you, don't make you the monster. You must plunge down with your hands and caress the roots of each tree. You triumph on that moss before you walk on it. You prune the hedges of the bushes and pick their sweetest fruit. No apologies. This is your kingdom. Care for your bonsai, your seedlings, your tiny, unfruiting grafts. Soon and even now you will be mighty. Soon and even now you will be moss, bush, and dwarf. The life is in you, golden, holy, held open and up and down and NOW. Even now. Forgive yourself and plant the seed of that greatness. It is going to grow whether or not you love it. Be the medicine you need. Make the love you want. Cry the prayers that lift you to God's cheek on the morning's climax. Forgive the nothingness of neglect, and the heaviness of malice. They are the manure of your greatest trees. Start with your own temple. Sweep out the cobwebs of dreams you put on pause because of that face someone made at your dream. Pray the prayer you need over someone else. Kill the shame with a mighty sword. And stand, royal, with your army of mighty trees.
There is therefore NOW
No condemnation

The Cry

No separation

No expiation

The bill is paid

The way is laid

Bare

Go

Grow

Be

·

Tiffany Vakilian

I Am Seeing Something

I feel totally happy even in a worn-out state because I know for the first time in a long time I'm ahead of the bullet
I'm not trying to catch it
I'm not riding on holding on for dear life I'm just there with my feet in front of it and it's pushing me somewhere faster than I can see
I have to trust and
I have to fly and
I'm so grateful that I am seeing something like this because
I cannot believe how long I've been holding back so I could feel comfortable and safe
But I can see something that looks like
Something

The Cry

Hurts

I hurt
inside my body as I heal
from my fourth cut
preparing and birthing
my son
my daughter
my son
I hurt
inside my heart
trying to understand the world
I want to teach my children to navigate
like a substrate
feeding on confusion and hate
I hurt
alone in this muddy, mixing
masturbation of waxy popularity
it's kinda nasty to me
I hurt
trying to keep down
my hurt and confusion
death and delusion
that my nuance will be in any way
accepted
bereft is
sort of a norm right now

Tiffany Vakilian

I hurt
fighting curses
Curse you mourning
morning and morning
my child, my family, my freedom
I hurt
so far down I can't even feel it anymore
rich and poor
with all these thoughts
just losing time
losing rhythm
I hurt
looking for the hurts
hurt
so I can purge and burn them out
purge and burn them
cauterized and cauterizing
scars
yes
even more scars
from broken promises and blatant neglect
but I have to give YOU what is left
of my good manners
good intentions
good feelings
I hurt
I can't
I hurt

The Cry

The Real Halo

What does it look like?
How do you and Moses play?
Holy controllers

How is the landscape?
What is heaven's gameplay goal?
Soon enough I'll know

But first I'll live out
Every destiny that's mine
And you will witness

Maybe that's the game
Being in the eternal
You play outside time

Tiffany Vakilian

Moses Tree

Just a trunk and some leaves

In some dirt

I don't even know

How you were buried

Was that wrong

I pour my love into your tree

I water it

Watch it grow

I symbolize you in the way

In my way

You touch my head with leaves

How tall and strong you are

It's not ok

But it is ok

It lives and gives me somewhere to

Pour my love for you

Hey Buttbutt,

The space you left when you left my body is still there. It bled for your sister and brother. Proof of the rainbow inside them. Proof of the war for them. Proof I am merely human. Proof my body knew what to do the whole time. The space you left is also still in my heart, often pressing on my hips. Mourning you is like hip surgery. Sutures of love are my scars.

The Cry

Used To

I used to be second born

Still am

I used to be second oldest

Not so much

I used to be mother of three

Still am

I used to have three living children

Not so much

I used to hide from my broken heart

Still am

I used to hide from my broken heart

Still am

I used to hide from my broken heart

Still am

I used to hide…

Not so much

Resources

There may be times when the subject matter or poetry may trigger the pain of a memory or emotional wound. You are not alone. If you need help, or someone to talk to, here are some resources to reach out to:

International Childbirth Association	800-624-4934
National Resource Center (Parenting/Relationships)	800-367-6724
National Sexual Assault Hotline	800-656-4673 (available 24 hours)
National Suicide Prevention Lifeline	Available 24/7 at 1-800-273-8255 You can also reach out for help by texting the word HOME to 741741
National Women's Health Information Center	800-994-WOMAN
M.E.N.D. Mommies Enduring Neonatal Death	www.mend.org/virtual-support-group-links
Parents Helping Parents (free self-help support groups)	800-882-1250
Postpartum Support International	800-944-4773 www.postpartum.net/get-help/loss-grief-in-pregnancy-postpartum
Postpartum Support International – Find Local Support	www.postpartum.net/get-help/locations

Guest Speaker

Tiffany Vakilian
www.speakfire.today

CEO and Founder of Speak Fire Publishing

Tiffany Vakilian is an entrepreneur with her Master's (and certification) in Transformative Language Arts. She is also an award-winning poet and performer committed to helping people use spoken, written, sung, or embodied word-art to facilitate social awareness and connection worldwide. Tiffany has a bold, yet tender style about her speaking that unlocks hidden stories within the audience, inspiring people to want to share those stories. She started SpeakFire Services to help unpublished authors go from holding their stories inside to confidently sharing polished, published books on the global stage.

Topics:
- *Need it, Want it, Deserve it* – Identity and Calling
- *Talents* – Identity and Calling
- *Understanding Editing* – Technical Expertise with Inspiration
- *Back From the Dead* – The Power of Story

Great For:
- Keynote
- Conferences
- Church Services
- Women's Retreats

Book to Speak:
Call 619-292-8772 or Email info@speakfire.today

Tiffany Vakilian

Also By Tiffany Vakilian

Books

Ugly Drawers, Pretty Panties:
A Collection of Poetry, Prose, Dreams and Missives

I Need to Stay Faithful, Else Y'all Gonna F.A.A.F.O.

Book Interior Basics:
A Guide for Independent or Self-Publishing Authors

Courses

Tiffany Vakilian's Manuscript to Market Process

The Book Interior Masterclass

Understanding Editing

www.ingramcontent.com/pod-product-compliance
Lightning Source LLC
Chambersburg PA
CBHW070341010526
44107CB00004B/579